How Artists Use
PATTERN AND TEXTURE

Paul Flux

Heinemann
LIBRARY

www.heinemann.co.uk

Visit our website to find out more information about Heinemann Library books.

To order:

 Phone 44 (0) 1865 888066

 Send a fax to 44 (0) 1865 314091

 Visit the Heinemann Bookshop at www.heinemann.co.uk to browse our catalogue and order online.

First published in Great Britain by Heinemann Library, Halley Court, Jordan Hill, Oxford OX2 8EJ, a division of Reed Educational and Professional Publishing Ltd.

Heinemann is a registered trademark of Reed Educational and Professional Publishing Ltd.

OXFORD MELBOURNE AUCKLAND JOHANNESBURG BLANTYRE
GABORONE IBADAN PORTSMOUTH (NH) USA CHICAGO

© Reed Educational and Professional Publishing Ltd 2002

Designed by Celia Floyd
Illustrations by Jo Brooker/Ann Miller
Originated by Ambassador Litho Ltd
Printed and bound by South China Printing in Hong Kong/China

ISBN 0 431 16201 8 (hardback)　　　　ISBN 0 431 16206 9 (paperback)
06 05 04 03 02　　　　　　　　　　　　06 05 04 03 02
10 9 8 7 6 5 4 3 2 1　　　　　　　　　　10 9 8 7 6 5 4 3 2 1

British Library Cataloguing in Publication Data

Flux, Paul
　　How artists use pattern and texture. (Take-off!)
　　1.Repetitive patterns (Decorative arts) in art – Juvenile literature 2.Repetitive patterns (Decorative arts)
　　Juvenile literature
　　I.Title
　　745.4

Acknowledgements

The publishers would like to thank the following for permission to reproduce photographs:

AKG, London: pp16, 24; Boomalli Aboriginal Artists: p12; Bridgeman Art Library: Arts Council Collection, Hayward Gallery, London p21, Alan Bowness Hepworth Estate / Bristol City Museum and Art Gallery p18, British Library, London p27, Christie's Images / Private Collection / DACS p9, Scottish National Gallery of Modern Art, Edinburgh / DACS p19, State Russian Museum, St. Petersburg p13; Trevor Clifford: p23; Corbis: pp7 bottom left, 20, Bojan Brecelj p5, Angelo Hornak p11, Matthew McKee, Eye Ubiquitous p15; M.C.Escher's *Metamorphosis 11* c.2000 Cordon Art B.V.-Baarn-Holland. All rights reserved: p22; Hunterian Art Gallery, University of Glasgow, Mackintosh Collection: p10; Oxford Scientific Films: pp6, 8; Photodisc: p7 top left and bottom right; SCALA: p28; V & A Picture Library: p26; Werner Forman Archive: pp4, 17; Woburn Abbey; p14.

Cover photograph reproduced with permission of Bridgeman Art Library/Arts Council Collection, Hayward Gallery, London.

Our thanks to Sue Graves and Hilda Reed for their advice and expertise in the preparation of this book.

Every effort has been made to contact copyright holders of any material reproduced in this book. Any omissions will be rectified in subsequent printings if notice is given to the publishers.

Contents

Any words appearing in the text in bold, **like this**, are explained in the Glossary.

What is a pattern?

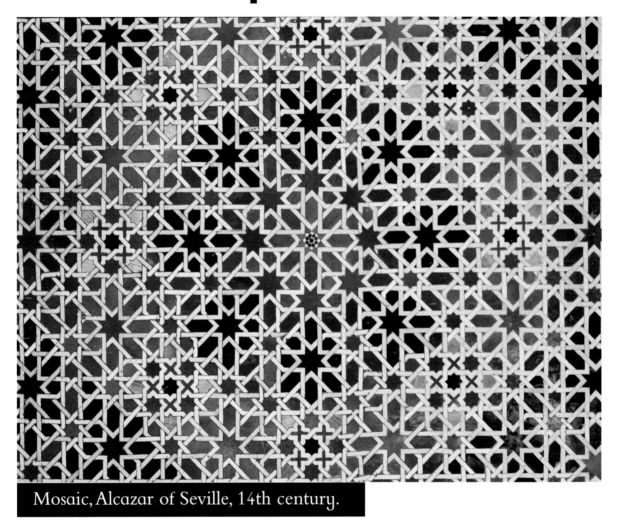

Mosaic, Alcazar of Seville, 14th century.

A pattern is a shape or **design** which is **repeated**. If you draw a simple shape, colour it and repeat it, you start to build a pattern. Patterns can be simple or complicated. Artists have used pattern for thousands of years, both to **decorate** and to add meaning to their work.

building   sign   vehicle

Chinatown, New York City, USA.

How many patterns can you find in this picture?

In the modern world patterns are everywhere. The signs, the shapes of the buildings and the vehicles in this picture all mix together to make a mass of pattern and colour. You can almost hear the noise!

Patterns and texture

Nature loves using pattern! We are surrounded by **designs**. Pattern can change how we see something. Plants can look like stones, insects can look like leaves!

Nature makes wonderful patterns like these.

stick insect

germander speedwell

butterfly fish

stone flowers

garter snake

These animals all have different textures.

swallowtail butterfly

tarantula

The way the surface of an object feels is called its **texture**. Many artists try to show how the things in their pictures would feel if you could really touch them.

Unusual patterns – nature in art

Wind and rain can wear rocks away at different rates. When this happens the effect is sometimes **dramatic**. Sandstone rocks can make colourful patterns in the changing light of day. These patterns have been cut over thousands of years and are still changing today.

sandstone rock

Rock formation, Colorado, USA.

Georgia O'Keeffe, *Out Back of Marie's*, 1930.

Georgia O'Keeffe has painted a **landscape** in which the folds of the rocks seem to be moving. It is as if the land is alive. The colours, **textures** and patterns the artist has used can all be found in nature, but she has mixed them together in her own, very special, way.

Man-made patterns

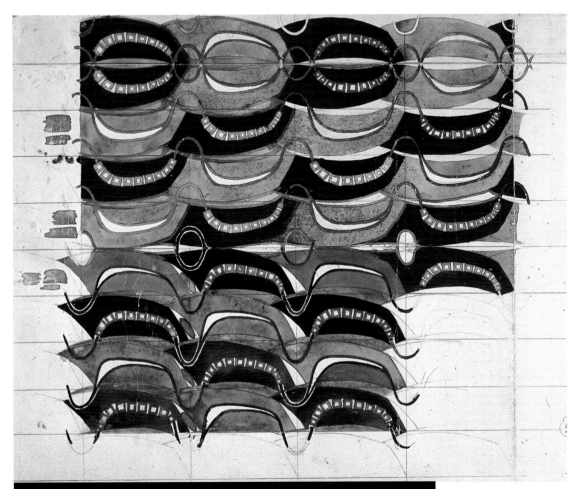

Charles Rennie Mackintosh, *Wave Pattern: Green, Purple, Pink, Orange and Black*, 1915-23.

The patterns of this **design** move from side to side, and also up and down. The artist has used a **grid** to help him make the pattern. Everywhere you look you can see shape, colour and line being **repeated** in this unusual design.

brick
pattern

chimney

Could
you design a
chimney pattern
yourself?

Patterns and **textures** can be found in the most unlikely of
places! This group of chimneys is at Hampton Court Palace, near
London. The palace was built nearly 500 years ago, when open
fires were the only way of heating a building. The palace has
dozens of chimneys and each one is different!

Shapes make patterns

The shape that is being **repeated** here is the **continent** of Australia. In between these shapes are **Aboriginal designs**, in black and white. The two parts of the pattern are very different from one another, but they do not **clash**.

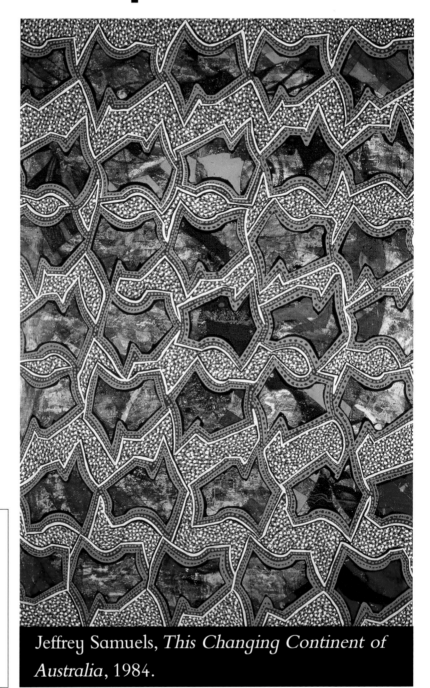

Jeffrey Samuels, *This Changing Continent of Australia*, 1984.

Can you see how the dotted black and white lines are used to make space in the picture?

Pavel Filonov, *Faces*, 1940.

In this picture patterns seem to move, and faces can be seen. Look carefully and you should be able to see three. The faces slowly appear from under the patterns and the eyes look straight at you. They seem trapped under the ever-moving shapes.

Patterns with meaning

Pattern can help make the meaning of a painting clear. Here is a **portrait** of Queen Elizabeth I, painted after England defeated the **Spanish Armada** in 1588. Look at her clothes! The fine pattern and **texture** of her dress tell us that this is a very powerful person who can afford expensive clothes, and an artist to paint her!

Artist unknown, *Elizabeth I Armada Portrait*, 1588.

Aboriginal man with painted face.

People have **decorated** their bodies for thousands of years. Often they do this to make themselves feel special. This **Aboriginal** man has painted his face with stripes and dots. Perhaps he is about to take part in a **ceremony**.

Patterns and texture in nature

birch tree

autumn leaves

Gustav Klimt was an Austrian artist. He lived from 1862 to 1918.

Gustav Klimt, *Birch Forest*, 1903.

Artists often try to copy the patterns they find in nature. Gustav Klimt painted this birch wood in autumn. He looked very hard at the patterns, **texture** and colour of the bark, and copied the huge range he had seen.

Not all patterns in nature are complicated. The delicate colours and shapes of these flowers have been perfectly copied by the artist. The leaves, flowers and stems are arranged simply across the picture. The picture makes you feel calm and peaceful.

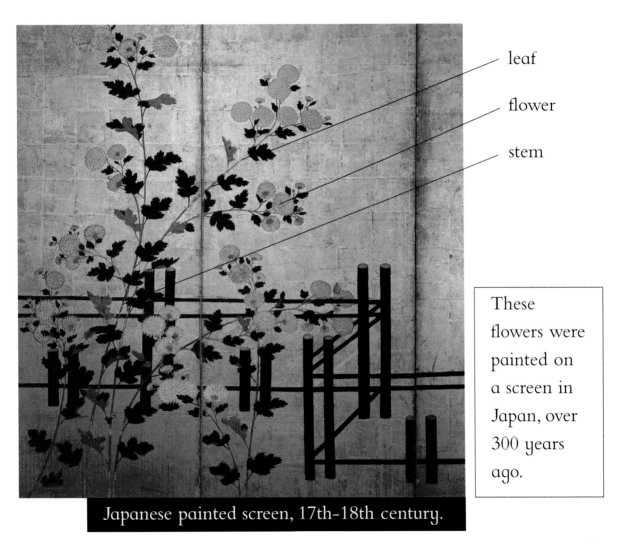

leaf

flower

stem

Japanese painted screen, 17th–18th century.

These flowers were painted on a screen in Japan, over 300 years ago.

Pattern at work

Barbara Hepworth made this picture just after the end of World War II (1939–45). This artist spent some time in a hospital and liked the work the **surgeons** did there. The five people stand in a row, all looking the same way. Three of the surgeons make a **repeated** pattern.

Barbara Hepworth, *The Hands*, 1948.

Fernand Léger was a French painter and designer. He lived from 1881 to 1955.

Fernand Léger, *Constructors: The Team at Rest*, 1950.

The French artist Fernand Léger painted this picture of men putting up a metal frame for a new building. The strong patterns and colours of the building frame support the men at work and those resting. The patterns in the building frame and the men's clothes give the picture a tough feel.

Pattern on the move

Yvaral Vasarely, *Untitled*, 1965.

In the 1960s, some artists became interested in the special effects that pattern and light can have on the eye. The pattern is the whole point of the painting, there is nothing else. Look at this for a while and the shapes can seem to move.

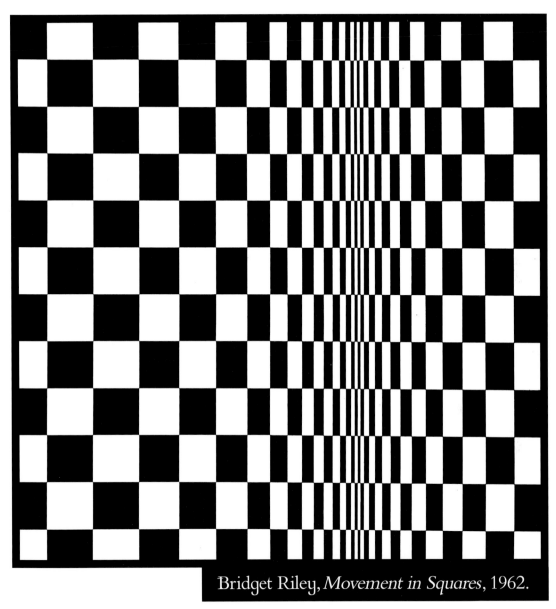

Bridget Riley, *Movement in Squares*, 1962.

Another artist who became interested in Op Art was the British painter Bridget Riley. She used just shape and line to make a number of pictures in black and white. Some are very hard to look at for long!

Bridget Riley was born in 1931. How old is she now?

Patterns that fit together

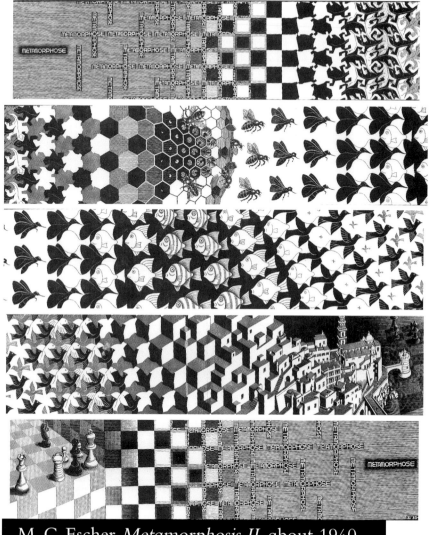

Shapes that fit together with no spaces in between are said to **tessellate**.

M. C. Escher, *Metamorphosis II*, about 1940.

This Dutch artist made many pictures with shapes that work together to make patterns. Look how the patterns and shapes change into each other in this very long picture.

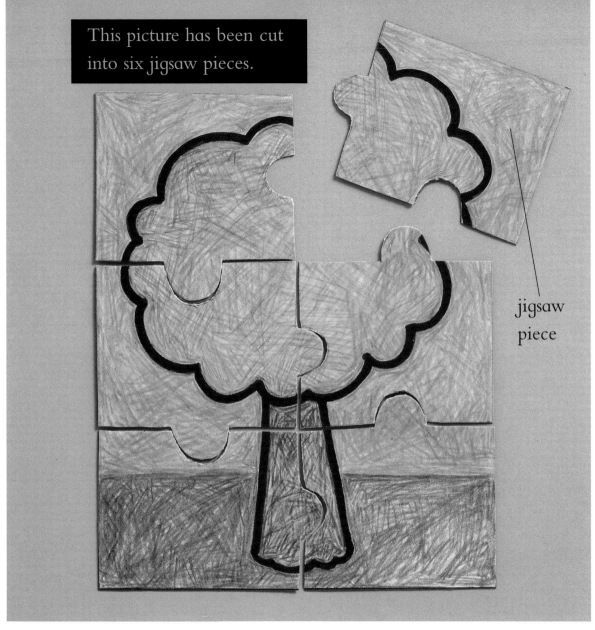

This picture has been cut into six jigsaw pieces.

jigsaw piece

Jigsaws are a kind of tessellation. Make your own like this.

1. Draw a pattern or a picture on some card.
2. Copy the shapes of the jigsaw pieces shown here onto your picture or make up your own shapes.
3. Cut out the picture pieces to make a jigsaw.

23

Pattern, colour and shape

The Russian artist Kasimir Malevich painted this picture.
He used simple shapes and only a few colours. We can see four
faceless people standing in line. Malevich wants to remind us of
Russian religious paintings, which often show saints in a line.

What do the patterned faces and bodies make you think of?

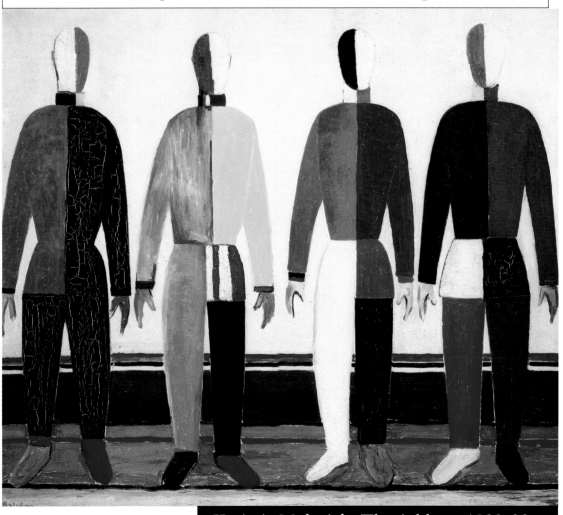

Kasimir Malevich, *The Athletes*, 1928–32.

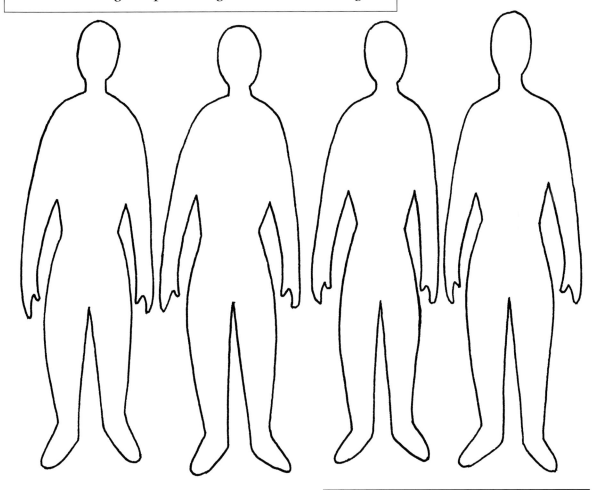

Have you found that you can put feeling into ordinary shapes using careful colouring?

Four figure outlines of people.

Here is the same picture without the colours. Try drawing your own people:

1. Copy the outlines onto a large piece of paper.
2. Colour them with your own patterns. Don't use too many colours and keep the patterns simple.
3. Colour part of the background as well.

25

Making pattern work for you

In this **stained glass design**, a woman is playing a lute. The artist has **divided** the space around the woman to look like tiles. The **repeated** pattern of daisies and sunflowers **decorates** the background in a quietly graceful way.

William Morris was an English artist who designed carpets, furniture, tiles and stained glass. He lived from 1834 to 1896.

sunflower   woman   lute   daisy

William Morris, *Woman Playing a Lute*, about 1872–74.

26

This pattern is simpler than it looks. Look carefully at the middle four squares (a **detail** is shown on the right) and you will see how the pattern fits together. Draw some squares and try making your own designs. Keep these simple at first, and make sure the corners match. Try putting a flower or plant in the centre.

This page is from a hand-painted book made more than 1300 years ago.

detail of the middle four squares

Page from the Lindisfarne Gospels, about AD 698.

Patterns old and new

Some of the oldest surviving patterns were made by the ancient Egyptians. This is the **sarcophagus** of Tutankhamun, made more than 3000 years ago. Red and blue glass has been put between lines of gold, to make a beautiful pattern. The Egyptians loved bright colours, and often gave their art patterned frames.

Tutankhamun was a king, or **pharaoh**, of Ancient Egypt. He was only about 11 years old when he became king! His coffin was made of solid gold.

gold line

blue glass

red glass

Sarcophagus of Tutankhamun, Egypt, about 1323 BC.

The next time you paint or draw a picture, put a patterned frame around it. Try some of these ideas.

1. Copy some of the squares below or **design** your own squares.
2. Use two or three different squares and **repeat** them to make a frame around your picture.
3. Use only a few colours, perhaps two for each square, to make a **decoration** just as good as the Egyptians made!

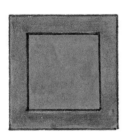
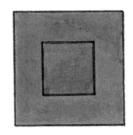
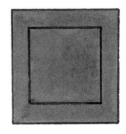

square patterns

repeat patterns

Design ideas for patterned frames.

Glossary

a b c d e f g h i j k l m n o p q r s t u v w x y z

Aboriginal   native person of Australia

architect   person who designs buildings

clash   colours look wrong together and hurt the eyes

ceremony   marching, dancing or another activity carried out on a special occasion

continent   mass of land on earth

decorate   make something more pleasant or interesting to look at

design   lines and shapes which decorate art

detail   part of a picture or design

divide   split into two or more parts

dramatic   something that is surprising or exciting

grid   pattern of regular lines

landscape   picture of natural and man-made scenery, for example, fields, trees and houses

mosaic   picture or pattern made with small coloured stones, glass or tiles

Op Art   short for Optical Art. A kind of painting in which lines and colour make the eyes see something which is not real, for example, pictures that look as if they move.

outline	line that shows the edge and shape of an object
pharaoh	king of Ancient Egypt
portrait	painting which shows what someone looks like
repeat	do something over and over again
sarcophagus	coffin
Spanish Armada	fleet of ships which sailed from Spain to invade England in 1588
stained glass	pieces of coloured glass put together to make a picture
style	the way in which a picture is painted
surgeon	doctor who performs operations in a hospital
tessellate	shapes which fit together with no spaces between them
texture	the feel or look of something

a
b
c
d
e
f
g
h
i
j
k
l
m
n
o
p
q
r
s
t
u
v
w
x
y
z

Index